glasswork

glasswork

Hand painting glass for the home

Mary Fellows
Photography by Michelle Garrett

southwater

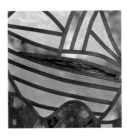

This edition is published by Southwater

Southwater is an imprint of
Anness Publishing Limited
Hermes House
88–89 Blackfriars Road
London
SE1 8HA
tel. 020 7401 2077
fax. 020 7633 9499

Distributed in the USA by
Anness Publishing Inc.
27 West 20th Street
Suite 504
New York
NY 10011
tel. 212 807 6739
fax. 212 807 6813

Distributed in the UK by
The Manning Partnership
251–253 London Road East
Batheaston
Bath BA1 7RL
tel. 01225 852 727
fax. 01225 852 852

Distributed in Australia by
Sandstone Publishing
Unit 1
360 Norton Street
Leichhardt
New South Wales 2040
Australia
tel. 02 9560 7888
fax. 02 9560 7488

3 5 7 9 10 8 6 4 2

Publisher: Joanna Lorenz
Editor: Sarah Ainley
Copy Editor: Beverley Jollands
Design: Penny Dawes
Photography: Michelle Garrett
Step Photography: Rodney Forte
Illustrators: Madeleine David and Lucinda Ganderton
Index: Helen Snaith
Editorial Reader: Jan Cutler
Production Controller: Steve Lang

CONTENTS

INTRODUCTION

Coloured glass has been a prized possession throughout the centuries for its beauty, whether it has been used as drinking glasses, ornaments or in windows. If you are lucky enough, as I am, to have a stained glass window in your home you will know how exquisite it is when the sunlight shines in. I forget about it most of the time as it only catches morning light, but the splash of colour it adds to the room is uplifting.

In this book we show you how to take clear glass and transform it with colour, adding your own distinctive details to create beautiful coloured glass. You can start with something as simple as painting a clip frame with a border for a print. The paint is easy to apply and as long as you use a paint specially formulated for use on glass, and follow the manufacturer's instructions, then the items you create can be used again and again. You won't need any specialist tools to get you started and you can decorate anything that is glass, from small plaques to hang at your window to wine glasses; or try painting on sheets of acetate to create your own birthday cards. We show how to paint freehand, add frosting to glasses and decorate simple Christmas baubles.

Each project is accompanied with clear step-by-step photography to guide you through each stage, and there are templates at the back of the book for any designs that you will need. There are also detailed instructions on how to prepare your glass and apply the paint. In no time at all you will be creating your own heirlooms.

Deborah Barker

FROSTED HIGHBALL GLASSES

Etching cream creates an elegant frosted effect which is perfect for glasses used for long, iced drinks. The delicate long-stemmed flowers are applied as reverse stencils: when the sticky-backed plastic is removed the clear glass motifs are revealed.

YOU WILL NEED
tracing paper
pencil
carbon paper
sticky-backed plastic
scissors
highball glasses
nail polish remover or glass cleaner
paper towels
rubber gloves
glass etching cream
medium paintbrush
warm water and sponge

1 Trace or draw freehand a simple flower, and use carbon paper to transfer it to the paper backing of a sheet of sticky-backed plastic.

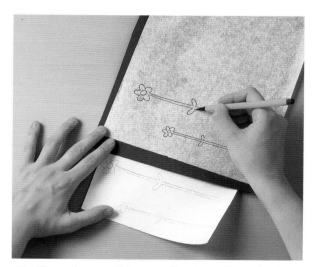

2 Draw the motif three to five times for each glass, depending on the size of the design.

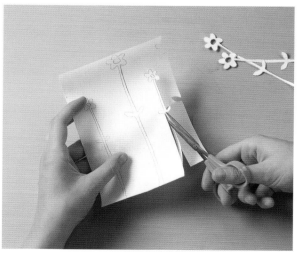

3 Cut out the motifs: use a pair of sharp-pointed scissors for any detailed shapes in the design. ▶

9

4 Clean the outside of each glass carefully, using nail polish remover or glass cleaner, to remove traces of grease and fingermarks.

5 Remove the backing paper from the motifs and stick them at regular intervals around the glass, varying the heights of the flowers. Trim the stems, if necessary, to add interest to the design.

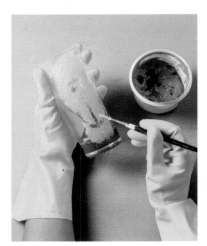

6 Wearing rubber gloves to protect your hands, paint the etching cream evenly over the outside of one glass. Leave the glass to dry in a warm, dust-free area for about 30 minutes.

7 Still wearing rubber gloves, wash the cream off the glass with warm water and let dry. For areas where the cream has not worked, paint the glass again and leave for another 30 minutes. Repeat with any remaining glasses.

8 Peel the sticky-backed plastic off the glass to reveal the motifs. Wash each glass again to remove any sticky smears caused by the plastic.

CHAMPAGNE FLUTES

Celebratory champagne bubbles were the inspiration for these decorated glasses. A fine mist of white paint, applied with a sponge, echoes the effervescence inside the glass, accentuated with a raised design of gold "bubbles" dotted up the sides.

YOU WILL NEED
clear glass champagne flutes
nail polish remover or glass cleaner
paper towels
flat paintbrush
glass paint: white
white ceramic tile or old plate
natural sponge
water or white spirit (paint thinner)
scrap paper
felt-tipped pen
gold relief outliner

1 Clean the champagne glasses carefully to remove any traces of grease and fingermarks. Using a flat paintbrush, apply a thin film of white glass paint over the surface of a ceramic tile or an old plate.

2 Moisten a sponge, using water if the glass paint is water-based or white spirit (paint thinner) if it is oil-based. Dab the sponge on to the paint on the tile.

3 Sponge white paint lightly on to the base, the stem and the lower part of the bowl of each champagne flute. Leave to dry thoroughly. ▶

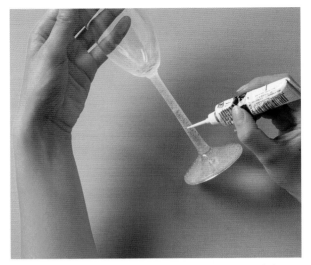

4 Draw around the base of one glass on a small piece of scrap paper to make a template. Fold the template into eighths, open it out and draw along the fold lines with a pen. Stand the glass on the template and dot along the guidelines using a gold outliner.

5 Dot gold outliner in a gradual spiral around the stem of the glass, turning the glass slowly as you work upwards.

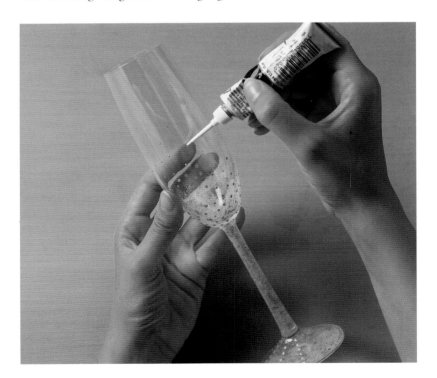

6 Dot the outliner on to the bowl of the glass, making the dots smaller and placing them further apart as you work up the glass. Place the final dots at least 2.5cm/1in below the rim so that they do not come in contact with the lips. Repeat with the remaining glasses. Bake the glasses in the oven to harden the paint if necessary, following the manufacturer's instructions.

BUTTERFLY BOWL

A flurry of butterflies and flowers covers the surface of this stunning bowl. They are painted freehand, with a few brushstrokes forming each wing or petal, and the decorative details are etched into the wet paint. Practise the shapes on a spare piece of glass first.

YOU WILL NEED
clear glass bowl
nail polish remover or glass cleaner
paper towels
tape measure
chinagraph pencil (china marker)
medium and fine paintbrushes
glass paints: grey, violet, mauve, bright pink,
pale blue and jade green
toothpick
cotton buds (swabs)

1 Clean the bowl. Measure down 5.5cm/2¼in from the rim of the bowl and mark the edge of the border with a chinagraph pencil (china marker). Divide the border into equal sections, 5.5cm/2¼in wide.

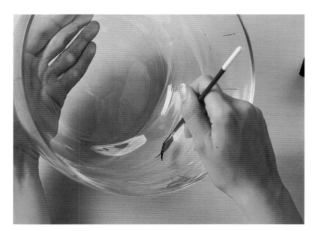

2 To paint a butterfly, use a rounded paintbrush for the body and apply a single brushstroke in grey paint. Use a fine paintbrush to paint the antennae.

3 Using violet paint, paint a pair of wings on each side of the body.

4 While the paint is still wet, use a toothpick to etch a simple design on the wings.

5 Paint butterflies at random all over the bowl below the border, using mauve paint for some of the wings, for variation.

6 To paint the flowers for the border, start with the centres, and paint a small circle in the middle of each section using mauve paint.

7 Paint five petals radiating out from each flower centre, using bright pink paint.

8 Etch a line along each flower petal using a toothpick. Leave to dry before progressing.

9 Below the border, fill in the areas between the butterflies with swirls of pale blue paint. Leave to dry.

10 Rub off the chinagraph pencil marks using cotton buds (swabs). Paint short wavy lines between the flowers around the border using jade green paint. Bake the glass to harden the paint if necessary, following the manufacturer's instructions.

HEART DECORATION

Craft suppliers stock a range of glassware especially for painting, and these small glass hearts would look beautiful catching the light as they twirl in a window. The decoration is a combination of frosting and raised metallic dots, applied to both sides of the glass.

YOU WILL NEED
clear glass heart shapes
nail polish remover or glass cleaner
paper towels
rubber gloves
glass etching cream
medium paintbrush
warm water and sponge
relief outliners: light gold, dark gold and bronze

1 Clean both sides of the glass shapes using nail polish remover or glass cleaner, to remove any traces of grease and fingermarks.

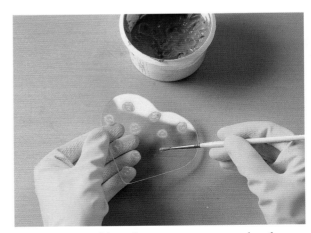

2 Wearing rubber gloves to protect your hands, paint etching cream in small circles at random all over one side of the glass. Leave to dry in a warm, dust-free area for about 30 minutes.

3 Still wearing rubber gloves, wash the cream off the glass with warm water, and leave to dry. If there are any areas where the cream has not worked, paint the glass again and leave for another 30 minutes.

4 Outline alternate etched circles using light gold outliner. Leave to dry.

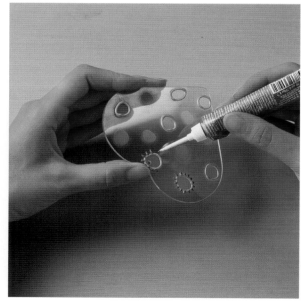

5 Add short "rays" all round each outline, using dark gold outliner.

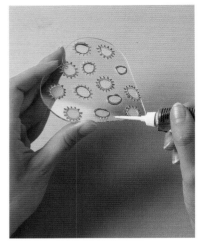

6 Outline the remaining circles using dark gold, then add rays in light gold. Leave to dry.

7 Use bronze outliner to add a few dots between the circles.

8 Turn the heart over and cover the etched areas in dots of bronze outliner. Leave to dry. Bake the glass to harden the paint if necessary, following the manufacturer's instructions.

CELEBRATION CARD

Glass paint and relief outliner can be used very successfully on acetate sheet, so you can use it to make unbreakable, lightweight decorations. Here, the painted design has been mounted in a card frame to make an original eighteenth birthday card.

YOU WILL NEED
scrap paper
pencil
acetate sheet
masking tape
relief outliners: silver or pewter, green,
pink and yellow
glass paints: yellow and white
medium paintbrush
paint tray
ruler
craft knife
cutting mat
stiff card (card stock)
all-purpose strong glue

1 Draw a simple freehand design on to scrap paper. Secure a piece of acetate over the drawing using masking tape.

2 Outline the number and both edges of the border using silver or pewter outliner. Leave to dry.

3 Draw a second line inside the outer border of each shape using green outliner.

4 Fill the numbers using pink outliner, and the border using yellow. Leave to dry.

5 Detach the acetate from the template and turn it over. Draw a pink outline just inside the border on the back of the sheet.

6 Mix yellow glass paint with white to make it opaque and fill in the square on the back of the design. Leave to dry.

7 Trim the acetate, leaving a border about 2.5cm/1in wide all round the design. Cut out a card in which to mount it, and measure and cut a window in the front of the card, about 5mm/¼in smaller all round than the acetate sheet.

8 Apply all-purpose strong glue around the window and glue the acetate sheet into the card.

CLIP FRAME

Cheap clip frames are widely available in almost any size you need, and you can give them real impact with painted borders. This one is decorated with relief outliner in a range of intense colours which have been dragged together while still wet to create an intricate yet orderly design.

YOU WILL NEED
clip frame
scrap paper
felt-tipped pen
ruler
nail polish remover or glass cleaner
paper towels
reusable adhesive
relief outliners: yellow, bright pink, green and orange
toothpick

1 Dismantle the frame and lay the glass on a sheet of scrap paper. Draw around the edge of the glass.

2 Divide the marked edge equally and draw a double border of squares around the template.

3 Clean the glass thoroughly with nail polish remover or glass cleaner to remove any traces of fingermarks and grease.

4 Attach the cleaned glass to the paper template using a small piece of reusable adhesive under each of the corners.

5 Using yellow outliner, trace the first square, drawing just inside the template guideline.

6 Using pink outliner, draw a second square just inside the first. Do not leave any gap between the lines.

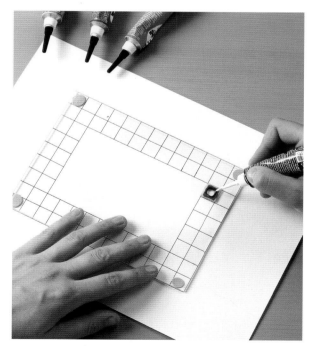

7 Draw a third line in the same way using green outliner. Draw carefully to avoid smudging the yellow and pink outliners.

8 Fill the centre of the square with the orange outliner, working in single strokes to avoid blending the orange with the green.

9 Working while the paint is still wet, use a toothpick to drag the colours from the corners of the square into the centre. Clean the excess paint from the toothpick with a paper towel after each stroke to keep the design neat.

10 Drag four more lines from the middle of each side of the square into the centre. Wipe the toothpick after each stroke, as before.

11 Repeat the technique on the next square: this time start with green, then use orange, pink and finally yellow in the centre.

12 Work around the border, alternating the two colour combinations. Leave the frame to dry. Bake the glass to harden the paint if necessary, following the manufacturer's instructions.

SUGAR SHAKER

Use the brightest colours in your paint collection for this extravagant design, then pile on even more decoration with spots and stripes in relief outliner. The horizontal bands of colour follow the ridged shape of the glass jar.

YOU WILL NEED
glass sugar shaker
nail polish remover or glass cleaner
paper towels
glass paints: white, bright pink, green, orange and blue
medium paintbrushes
paint tray
relief outliners: dark gold, light gold, pink, blue, bronze and green

1 Remove the metal top of the shaker and clean the outside of the glass thoroughly, using nail polish remover or glass cleaner, to remove any traces of grease and fingermarks.

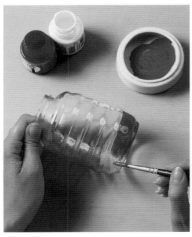

2 Add a little white glass paint to each colour to make them opaque. Paint the bottom band of the shaker bright pink.

3 Paint the next band green. Use the ridges in the glass as guidelines for the painted band.

4 Leave the next ridge of the jar unpainted and then paint a band of orange.

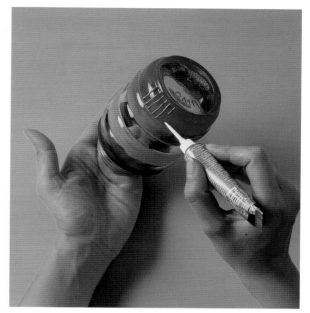

5 Leave the next ridge unpainted. Paint the top band of the jar with blue paint, then leave the paint to dry.

6 Using outliner, draw vertical dark gold lines across the pink band all round the bottom of the shaker, and small light gold circles around the green band.

7 Using pink outliner, make a double staggered row of dots around the lower unpainted band.

8 Using the blue outliner, add a large dot of paint inside each gold circle.

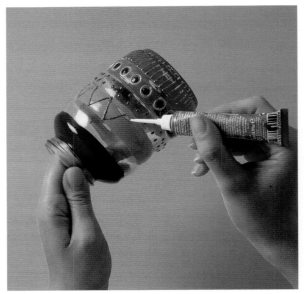

9 Using the bronze outliner, draw zigzags all the way round the orange band.

10 Using the green outliner, draw vertical crosses around the upper unpainted band.

11 Next, draw an even number of light gold vertical lines around the blue band.

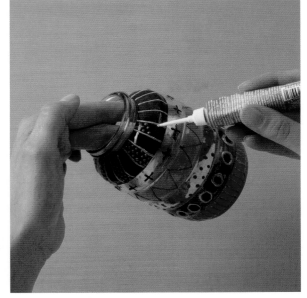

12 Using the dark gold outliner, fill alternate spaces between the gold lines with tiny dots. Let the paint dry. Bake the glass to harden the paint if necessary, following the manufacturer's instructions.

SEASHELL LOTION DISPENSER

Decorated with a marine theme, this pretty bottle will look good on a bathroom shelf. It is scattered with reversed-stencilled seashell shapes and delicately sponged with pale, opaque paints inspired by the shimmering colours of mother-of-pearl.

YOU WILL NEED
clear glass lotion dispenser
masking tape (optional)
nail polish remover or glass cleaner
paper towels
felt-tipped pen
thin cardboard (card stock)
cutting mat
craft knife
sticky-backed plastic
white ceramic tile or old plate
glass paints: white, jade green, mauve and bright pink
flat paintbrush
natural sponge
water or white spirit (paint thinner)

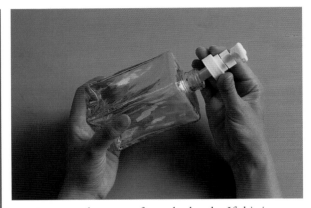

1 Remove the pump from the bottle. If this is not possible, cover it with masking tape to protect it from the paint. Clean the bottle carefully to remove traces of grease and fingermarks.

2 Copy the shell templates from the back of the book on to cardboard (card stock). Cut them out and draw around them on the paper backing of a sheet of sticky-backed plastic. Make a total of about ten motifs, depending on the size of the lotion dispenser.

3 Using a craft knife and working on a cutting mat, carefully cut out the shell motifs.

4 Peel off the paper backing and stick the shell motifs in a random but even pattern around the sides of the lotion dispenser.

5 On a white tile or old plate, mix white and jade green paint together. Brush a thin film of paint over the tile using a flat paintbrush.

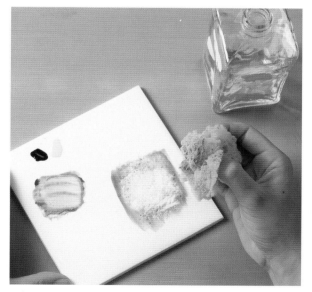

6 Moisten a natural sponge with water if using water-based paints or white spirit (paint thinner) for oil-based paints. Dab at the paint with the sponge.

7 Sponge the light green paint very lightly all over the lotion dispenser. Leave it to dry completely.

▶

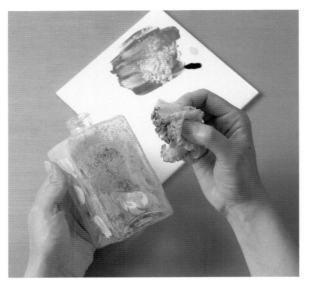

8 Mix white and mauve paint together and sponge it on in the same way, allowing the light green colour underneath to show through.

9 Mix white and bright pink paint together and sponge it on to the lotion dispenser as before, allowing the green and mauve paints to show through.

10 Leave the paint to dry, then peel off the plastic shapes. Bake the glass to harden the paint if necessary, following the manufacturer's instructions (do not bake if the pump is still in place). If the pump was removed, replace the fitting, or peel off the masking tape.

GLASS JAR LANTERN

Ordinary glass jars make useful windproof containers for candles, to light the garden during summer evenings; using glass paints, you can turn them into magical lanterns. Look out for interesting and unusual shapes, with facets or ridges to enhance your design.

YOU WILL NEED
glass jar
nail polish remover or glass cleaner
paper towels
black relief outliner
tape measure
chinagraph pencil (china marker)
tape reel
glass paints: red and orange
medium and fine paintbrushes
toothpick (optional)
fine wire
wire cutters
8 beads
round-nosed pliers

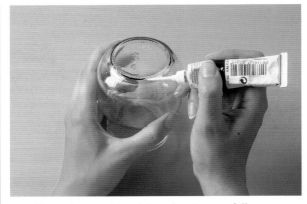

1 Clean the outside of the glass jar carefully to remove traces of grease and fingermarks, then stand it upside down and draw a line all the way around the base using the black relief outliner.

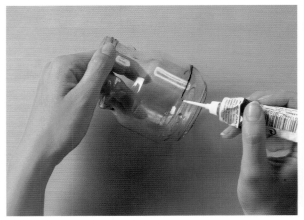

2 Measure 2cm/¾in up from the base of the glass jar and mark this level using a chinagraph pencil (china marker). Use the outliner to draw a horizontal line around the jar following the reference mark. Draw two more horizontal lines at 2cm/¾in intervals.

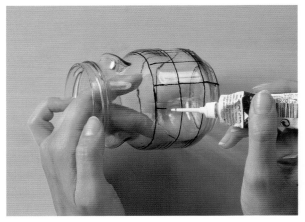

3 Measure around the jar and mark 2cm/¾in intervals with the chinagraph pencil. Using these marks for reference, draw vertical lines with the outliner to divide the rings into squares. Leave to dry.

4 Support the jar on its side on a tape reel to stop it from rolling around as you work. Paint one of the squares with red paint.

5 Using the end of a fine paintbrush or a toothpick, etch a small star in the centre of the red square. Wipe the paint off the brush after each stroke.

6 Paint the next square orange and etch a star as before. Paint and decorate all the squares, alternating the colours. Work only on the uppermost area so that the paint does not run, and wait for the paint to dry before turning the jar to continue.

7 Bake the glass to harden the paint if necessary, following the manufacturer's instructions. Meanwhile, cut a 30cm/12in length of wire to make a handle and thread the beads on to it.

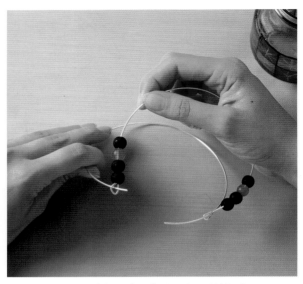

8 Use a pair of round-nosed pliers to bend each end of the wire into a small loop.

9 Cut a second length of wire 3cm/1¼in longer than the circumference of the glass jar. Thread it through the loops in the handle.

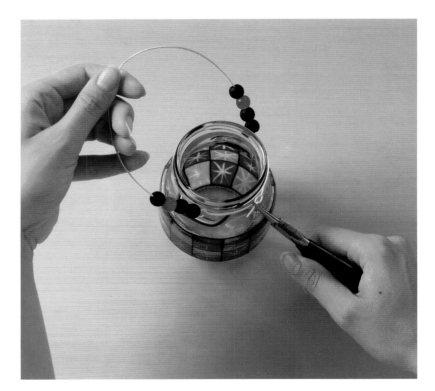

10 Wrap the shorter wire around the neck of the jar below the screw thread. Adjust the handle so that the loops are opposite one another. Bend one wire end into a loop and thread the other end through it. Pull it tight, then bend it back and squeeze the hooks closed. Always take care with candles and never leave a burning candle unattended.

CHRISTMAS BAUBLES

For this year's Christmas tree, buy plain glass baubles and decorate them yourself to make beautiful, completely original ornaments. They look lovely at every stage, so just take the decoration as far as you wish, or vary the design with stencils of different shapes.

YOU WILL NEED
clear glass baubles
nail polish remover or glass cleaner
paper towels
self-adhesive labels: small spots
glass etching spray
paper clips
gold relief outliner
fine glitter
scrap paper
glass paint: bright yellow
fine paintbrush

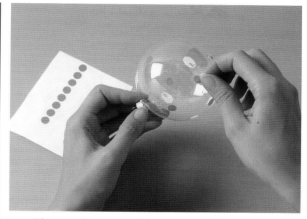

1 Clean each glass bauble very carefully to remove traces of grease and fingermarks, then stick the self-adhesive paper spots all over it, spacing them evenly in a balanced design.

2 Spray on an even coat of glass etching medium, following the manufacturer's instructions. Hang the bauble up to dry, using a paper clip as a hook. Leave for about 45 minutes.

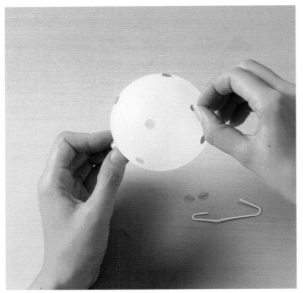

3 Peel off the paper spots and discard. Clear circles will be revealed all over the bauble.

4 Outline each circle with gold relief outliner, then draw a second circle around the first. Add some squiggly lines radiating from the neck of the bauble.

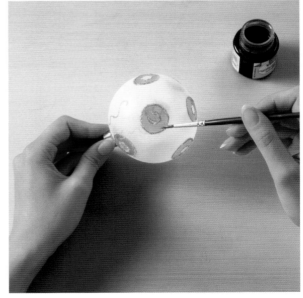

5 While the outliner is still wet, sprinkle it with glitter, holding the bauble over a sheet of paper to catch the excess. Hang the bauble up to dry.

6 Fill in-between the inner and outer rings with glass paint in bright yellow, and hang the bauble up to dry. Repeat for any remaining baubles.

VENETIAN PERFUME BOTTLE

This enchanting bottle, with its swags of little dots and pretty gilded flowers, is reminiscent of 19th-century Italian enamelled glassware. Use opaque ceramic paints for this project so that the tiny details show up clearly in delicate relief.

YOU WILL NEED
round clear glass bottle
nail polish remover or glass cleaner
paper towels
tracing paper
scrap paper
scissors
chinagraph pencil (china marker)
opaque ceramic paints: white, red and gold
fine paintbrush
cotton buds (swabs)

1 Clean the bottle. Trace the template at the back of the book, adjusting it to fit eight times around the bottle, then cut out the two scallop shapes. Use a chinagraph pencil (china marker) to draw round scallop A eight times, fitting it close to the neck of the bottle. Draw in the curls, then draw around scallop B, fitting it between the first scallops.

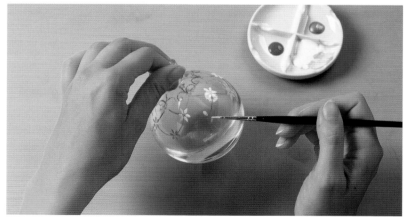

2 Using white paint, paint a six-petalled daisy at the bottom of each upper scallop. Mix a little red paint with white, and paint eight pale pink daisies at the base of each lower scallop.

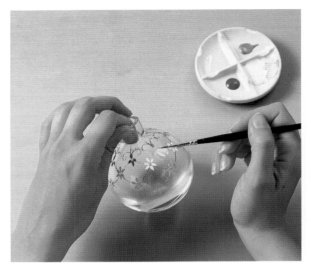

3 Using the template design as a guide, paint a four-petalled flower in gold paint between each scallop in the first round. Then fill in the centres of the daisies in gold paint.

4 Using the fine paintbrush, add tiny dots of white, gold and pink paint in delicate swags and lines to link the flowers.

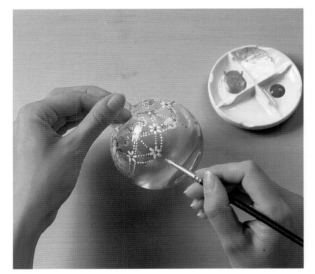

5 Fill in the gold ovals and pink and white dots at the top of each heart shape, then complete the design with two small gold dots at the base of each pink daisy. Extend the design with rows of tiny dots up the neck of the bottle.

6 Paint a large pink daisy in the centre of the bottle stopper. Add a gold centre and rows of tiny white dots radiating from the petals. Leave the paint to dry, then rub off the pencil marks using a cotton bud (swab). Bake the glass to harden the paint if necessary, following the manufacturer's instructions.

STAINED GLASS WINDOW

This impressive panel is in the style of the "leaded lights", or pictorial windows, which were fashionable adornments for front doors and porches in the late 1930s. A gallant ship tossed on huge waves was one of the most popular subjects.

YOU WILL NEED
pane of glass to fit window
nail polish remover or glass cleaner
paper towels
scrap paper
felt-tipped pen
reusable adhesive
adhesive lead strip
tin snips or old scissors
boning peg or teaspoon
craft knife
glass paints: red, yellow, turquoise, dark blue, white
medium and fine paintbrushes
paint tray

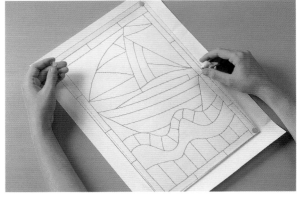

1 Clean the glass, using nail polish remover or glass cleaner. Draw a ship with hull and sails and waves on scrap paper to fit your panel and attach it to the underside of the glass using reusable adhesive.

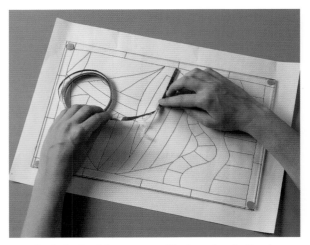

2 Peel the backing paper off a length of adhesive lead strip and lay it over the lines of the design, beginning with the hull of the boat.

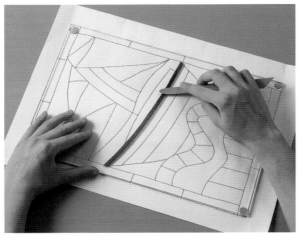

3 Trim the end of the lead strip at the end of the line, and smooth it down firmly using a boning peg or the back of a teaspoon, to ensure a good contact with the glass.

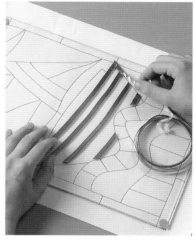

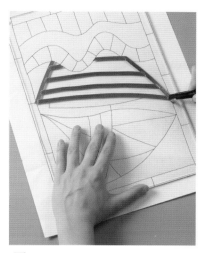

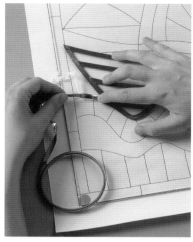

4 Repeat for the rest of the planks of the hull. Complete the outline of the boat, laying the strips over the ends of the previous ones.

5 Trim the ends of the outline, and smooth down with the boning peg or teaspoon.

6 Next, attach the lead strips for the waves of the sea, laying down the long strips first. Ease the strips carefully around the curves of the waves, using your fingers.

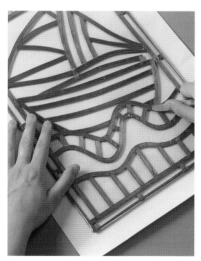

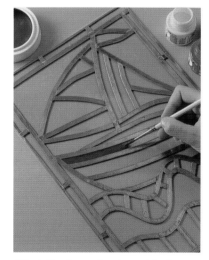

7 Complete the boat mast, sails and frame in the same way. Burnish all the lines with the boning peg, carefully smoothing down the fullness on the inside of the curves.

8 Mix the red paint with the yellow and a touch of the dark blue to give a burnt orange colour. Paint the top plank of the hull with the orange colour.

9 For the next plank, mix the red with more yellow to make a brighter orange. Add more yellow still to make a light orange for the third plank, and paint the lowest plank yellow.

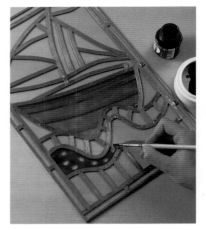

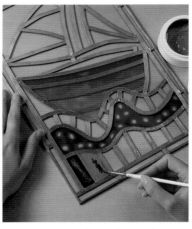

10 Fill in the central wave with the turquoise paint, leaving small randomly spaced circles of clear glass.

11 Use the dark blue paint to paint around the edge of the first panel in the lowest part of the sea. Mix dark blue with white, and paint a pale blue strip down the middle of the panel while the dark blue is still wet. Draw the edges of the two colours together to give a marbled effect.

12 Repeat in each panel, alternating the order of the colours. Paint alternate panels in the top wave dark or pale blue, leaving the remaining panels clear.

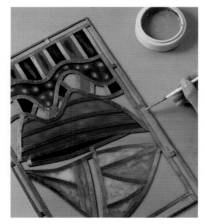

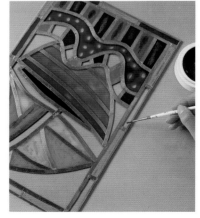

13 Mix red with dark blue to make purple, and paint the cabin roof. Paint alternate panels of the sails yellow, then add a little blue to make light green for the remaining parts of the sails.

14 Mix white with the light green and paint alternate panels of the frame. Paint the flag with the red paint.

15 Mix turquoise with the pale blue for the remaining panels of the frame. Leave the panel to dry completely.

MOSAIC VASE

The abstract design on this vase is applied just as if it were really a mosaic. Instead of squares of coloured glass, the "tesserae" are cut out of acetate sheet, painted in a selection of clear colours. The slight irregularities in the hand-cut squares give the decoration a lovely spontaneity.

YOU WILL NEED
clear glass tank-shaped vase
nail polish remover or glass cleaner
paper towels
acetate sheet
scissors
scrap paper
ruler
glass paints: yellow, red, blue, lime green and dark green
flat paintbrush
paint tray
all-purpose strong glue

1 Clean the glass. Cut five pieces of acetate sheet. (Measure the sheet against the sides of the vase to estimate how much you will need.)

2 Lay the acetate on a piece of scrap paper and paint with a wash of yellow glass paint, using a flat brush and applying all the strokes in one direction.

3 Mix some yellow into the red paint to make a deep orange. Paint the whole of each piece of acetate in one of the colours of the design. Leave the paint to dry thoroughly.

4 Cut each piece of painted acetate into 1cm/½in strips and set the strips aside in piles.

5 Cut the strips into 1cm/½in squares, keeping the different colours in separate piles.

6 Pick up the first green square on the tip of your finger and dab a little glue on to it.

7 Glue a line of squares in alternate greens across the bottom of the vase, to give a mosaic effect. ▷

8 Glue a line of yellow squares above the green squares to make the second row.

9 Glue a square of four orange pieces above the yellow line to vary the pattern.

10 Glue a square of blue pieces beside the orange square, then repeat the pattern. Add a second line of yellow squares, then a line of blue, orange and lime green squares in a repeating sequence.

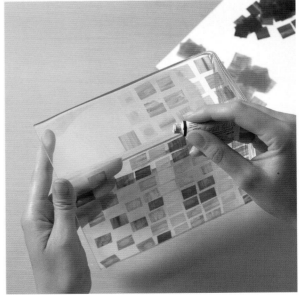

11 Complete the design with a random mixture of greens, leaving gaps between the squares. Continue the pattern on the other sides of the vase.

DOOR NUMBER PLAQUE

Transparent glass paints are available in a lovely range of rich colours, which you can combine for a jewel-like effect in pieces like this number plaque, where they are set off by the dark outline of the leading just as in a real stained glass window.

YOU WILL NEED
tracing paper
pencil
carbon paper
plain paper
black felt-tipped pen
square glass pane with polished edges
nail polish remover or glass cleaner
paper towels
adhesive lead strip
tin snips or old scissors
boning peg or teaspoon
glass paints: bright green, yellow, maroon, turquoise and dark blue
medium paintbrushes

1 Trace a favourite flower pattern and add the appropriate number. Use carbon paper to transfer the design to a sheet of plain paper.

2 Draw over the lines of the transferred design using a black felt-tipped pen.

3 Clean the glass carefully, using nail polish remover or glass cleaner, to remove any traces of grease and fingermarks.

4 Place the design under the glass as a guide for applying the adhesive lead strip. Apply the strips of lead for the number, then the flowers, leaves and stems. Ease the lead carefully around the curves, using your fingers.

5 Use a boning peg or the back of a teaspoon to rub down the lead strip to ensure that it makes a good contact with the glass.

6 Paint the leaves using bright green paint. Paint carefully within the lead strips and wipe off any mistakes with nail polish remover and paper towels.

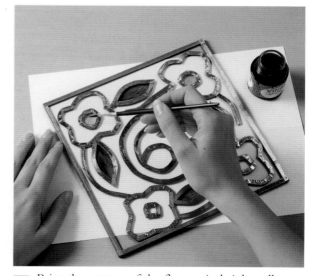

7 Paint the centres of the flowers in bright yellow. Take care not to smudge the green paint as you work around the plaque. ▶

8 Paint the petals of the flowers with the maroon paint, wiping off any mistakes as before.

9 Paint the central circle around the house number in bright turquoise.

10 Paint the background in dark blue. Leave the paint to dry completely.

TRINKET BOX

Small plastic boxes with well-fitting lids can be used to keep all kinds of small treasures safe.
Next time you acquire one as the packaging around chocolates or toiletries, recycle it with style,
jazzing it up with strong colours and a sprinkling of tiny, glittering seed beads.

YOU WILL NEED
clear plastic box
black relief outliner
ruler
flat-backed gold bead
all-purpose glue
small glass beads
glass paints: dark brown, crimson and yellow
medium and fine paintbrushes
paper towels

1 Mark out a simple geometric pattern on the lid of the box, using black relief outliner. Use a ruler to keep the lines straight.

2 Rest the outliner on the ruler to guide it when you are outlining the edge of the lid.

3 While the outliner is still wet, press a flat-backed gold bead into the centre. As it dries, the outliner will hold the bead securely in place.

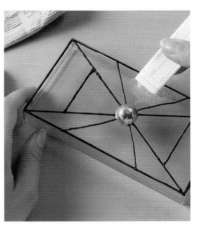

4 Cover the four panels on the cross on the lid with a thin layer of all-purpose glue.

5 While the glue is wet, sprinkle small glass beads on to the surface and let them stick.

6 Fill in the areas between the beaded panels using the dark brown glass paint.

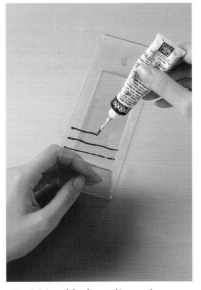

7 Paint the remaining areas on top of the lid in crimson.

8 Paint the sides of the lid in crimson, and leave to dry.

9 Using black outliner, draw vertical lines down the sides of the box at 1cm/½in intervals. ▶

10 Immediately, drag the pointed end of a paintbrush through the lines to break them up. Drag the brush in alternate directions at 1cm/½in intervals down the sides, wiping the excess paint off the brush at the end of each stroke. Leave for at least an hour to dry.

11 Use a fine paintbrush to paint alternate stripes in crimson along the side of the box.

12 Paint the remaining stripes in bright yellow and leave to dry completely.

LEAF PHOTOGRAPH FRAME

The decoration on this double-layered glass frame has been painted on the inside of the glass. This means that you need to paint the details on the leaves first, and the background colour second. Remember to reverse the template.

YOU WILL NEED
tracing paper
double-layer glass clip frame
scissors
masking tape
felt-tipped pen
nail polish remover or glass cleaner
paper towels
fine and medium paintbrushes
glass paints: dark and light green
photograph (optional)

1 Cut a piece of tracing paper the same size as the frame. Using small tabs of masking tape, stick your chosen photograph in place. Mark its position, then draw a selection of leaves around the photograph, following the templates at the back of the book.

2 Thoroughly clean the glass that forms the front of the frame. Remove the photograph and turn the tracing paper back-to-front. Attach it to the glass using masking tape.

3 Using a fine paintbrush, fill in the leaf stems of the design with the dark green paint.

4 Again using dark green, fill in the small triangles that represent the veins in the leaves. Leave the paint to dry completely.

5 Paint the leaf shapes in light green. Leave to dry, then remove the template. Bake the glass to harden the paint if necessary, following the manufacturer's instructions.

6 Attach the photograph to the second glass sheet, checking its position against the marks on the template. Assemble the frame.

MONOGRAMMED WINE GLASS

White glass paint is opaque and can be used to create an etched effect. Using a foolproof stencil technique, it's easy to decorate a wine glass with a classic monogram to make an elegant personalized gift for someone special.

YOU WILL NEED

pencil and plain paper or computer and printer

scissors

ruler

wine glass

nail polish remover or glass cleaner

paper towels

masking tape

clear sticky-backed plastic

soft cloth

craft knife

glass paint: white

1 Draw or print out your chosen initials to the size required for the glass. Cut out the initials leaving a 1cm/½in margin all round.

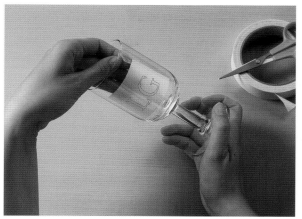

2 Clean the outside of the glass carefully, using nail polish remover or glass cleaner, to remove any traces of grease and fingermarks. Position the template inside the glass and secure with masking tape.

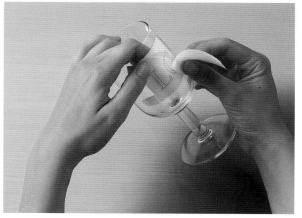

3 Cut a rectangle of clear sticky-backed plastic which is large enough to cover the letters. Remove the backing paper and stick it to the front of the glass. Smooth with a soft cloth to ensure that it adheres properly. ▶

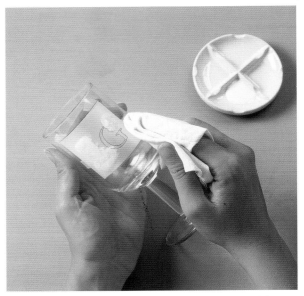

4 Using a sharp craft knife, cut out the initials following the outlines exactly. Peel away the plastic inside the letters to make the letter stencil.

5 Apply white glass paint over the stencil, dabbing it on with a soft cloth to create a frosted look.

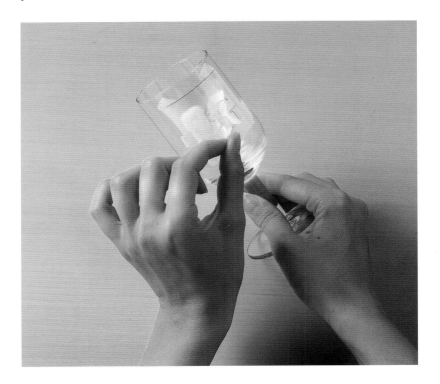

6 Peel off the letter stencil carefully. Leave the painted letters to dry completely, then bake the glass if necessary to harden the paint, following the manufacturer's instructions.

BOHEMIAN BOTTLE

Some mineral water is sold in bottles that are too beautiful to discard. This elegantly shaped blue one has been recycled with a decoration inspired by a 19th-century original found in an antique shop.

YOU WILL NEED
tracing paper
pencil
scissors
blue bottle
nail polish remover
or glass cleaner
paper towels
masking tape
chinagraph pencil
(china marker)
ceramic paints:
gold, white, green,
red and yellow
medium and fine
paintbrushes
paint tray

1 Trace the template at the back of the book and cut out the bold centre section. Clean the bottle to remove any traces of grease and fingermarks. Tape the template to the bottle and draw round it using a chinagraph pencil (china marker).

2 Fill in the shape with several coats of gold paint, stippling it on to create a textured effect.

3 Using white paint and a fine brush, outline the shape and add swirls along the top edge. ▶

4 Mix white with a little green paint and shade the border design with touches of pale green.

5 Paint the green leaves with loose brushstrokes, and add highlights in pale green. Draw in the red and yellow dots along the curves of the white border and for the flower centres.

6 Paint in the daisy petals using white paint. Add three small hearts and one or two small yellow flowers to the design for decorative detail.

FRENCH-LAVENDER FLOWER VASE

Spiky stems of French lavender, with their picturesque winged flower-heads, criss-cross over the front of this beautiful vase. Opaque paints have been used to give the flowers solidity and impact against the clear glass, above the subtle gleam of the gold stems.

YOU WILL NEED
tracing paper
felt-tipped pen
scissors
masking tape
straight-sided glass vase
nail polish remover or glass cleaner
paper towels
ruler
opaque ceramic paints: gold, white, purple, crimson and green
paint tray
high-density synthetic sponge
medium and fine paintbrushes

1 Trace the template at the back of the book, enlarging it as necessary to fit the vase. Use masking tape to attach the tracing to the inside of the glass. Clean the outside of the vase to remove traces of grease and fingermarks.

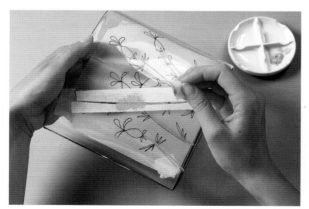

2 Draw a shallow curve along a length of masking tape and cut along it. Stick the two parts to the vase, following one of the stems on the template and leaving a 3mm/⅛in space between them. Sponge gold paint along the stem and leave to dry. Peel off the tape and repeat for the other stems.

3 Mix white with purple paint and fill in the teardrop shapes for the flower-heads in light purple. Add darker shades of purple and crimson towards the bottom of each flower, stippling the paint to create texture.

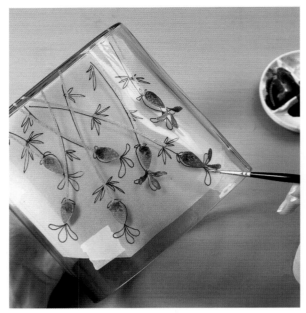

4 Paint the three petals at the top of each flower in pale purple, using long, loose brushstrokes. Leave the paint to dry.

5 Indicate the individual florets on each flower-head with small oval shapes in dark purple. Leave the paint to dry.

6 Using a fine paintbrush, draw spiky leaves along the stems in two or three shades of dusky green. Leave to dry, then bake the vase to harden the paint if necessary, following the manufacturer's instructions.

CRAZY-PAVING MIRROR

Pieces of mirror mosaic and lead strip make an easy and unusual three-dimensional frame for a plain mirror. As an alternative to using mirror mosaic, you can create a similar design by drawing the squares with relief outliner before painting around them.

YOU WILL NEED
mirror with polished edges
nail polish remover or glass cleaner
paper towels
mirror mosaics
glue gun and glue sticks
adhesive lead strip
tin snips or old scissors
boning peg or teaspoon
glass paints: turquoise and dark blue
medium paintbrush
black relief outliner (optional)
ruler (optional)
sticky-backed plastic or masking tape (optional)

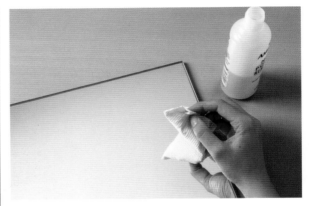

1 Clean the mirror carefully, using nail polish remover or glass cleaner, to remove traces of grease and fingermarks.

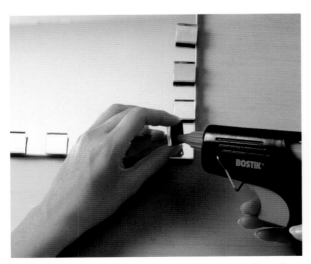

2 Arrange pieces of mirror mosaic around the edge of the mirror, spacing them evenly. When you are satisfied with the arrangement, glue each one in place using a hot glue gun.

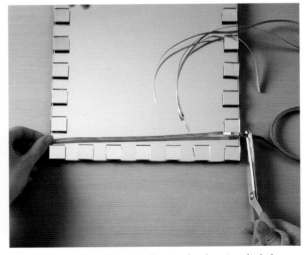

3 Cut four lengths of adhesive lead strip, slightly longer than the four sides of the mirror. The excess can be trimmed later.

4 Remove the backing paper and stick the strips in place to form the inner border of the frame.

5 Burnish the lead with a boning peg or teaspoon to ensure a good contact with the glass, and trim.

6 Using turquoise glass paint, paint the background of the frame sides, between the mosaic pieces.

7 Fill in the four corners of the mirror with the dark blue paint.

▶

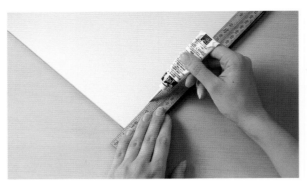

8 To paint the alternative design, draw the inner border in black outliner, using a ruler to keep the lines straight.

9 Mark out the design with squares of sticky-backed plastic or masking tape and outline the squares in black. Leave to dry.

10 Paint the sides of the border in turquoise and the corners in dark blue, leaving the squares unpainted. Leave to dry.

MATERIALS

Glass painting requires very few specialist materials. Start with a small collection of paints and add colours as you need them. You can use empty glass bottles and jars salvaged from the kitchen and bathroom to practise on.

ACETATE SHEET (1)

Glass-painting techniques can be used very effectively on clear acetate, which is available in various thicknesses, to make greetings cards and decorations.

ADHESIVE LEAD STRIP (2)

This self-adhesive strip is sold on a reel and can be used to reproduce the effect of stained glass on windows and mirrors. Ensure a good seal with the glass by burnishing the lead with a special tool called a boning peg, which is sometimes supplied with the reel, or the back of a teaspoon. Do not smoke or handle food while working with lead, and keep it out of reach of children. Wash your hands after handling it.

GLASS ETCHING CREAM (3)

This gives glass a frosted surface, and is best used with stencils made from sticky-backed plastic, which stick to the glass to ensure that the cream does not seep under the edges. Brush it on evenly and leave to dry in a warm, dust-free place for 30 minutes, then wash off with warm water. Always wear rubber gloves to protect your hands. Etching sprays are available as an alternative to the cream.

PAINTS (4)

Transparent glass paints are available in vivid colours. Most look quite dark in their containers, so it is a good idea to paint a sample of each colour on a spare piece of glass to act as a reference. The colours can be mixed, but use colourless glass paint to lighten transparent colours, as white is opaque. If you want an opaque effect, ceramic paints can also be used on glass. Both oil-based and water-based glass paints are available: the two types should not be combined. Let painted glass dry for at least a week before washing it. Some paints can be hardened in the oven to make them tough and dishwasher-proof: follow the paint manufacturer's instructions.

RELIEF OUTLINER (5)

Acrylic paste relief outliner comes in a range of colours and metallic finishes and can be used decoratively on its own or piped around a design to make a raised outline, forming a reservoir to contain the glass paint.

EQUIPMENT

Ordinary painting and drawing implements such as paintbrushes, chinagraph pencils (china markers) and sponges are all you will need for glass painting, and these are widely available from general art and craft suppliers.

ADHESIVES (1)
Use masking tape or reusable adhesive to attach templates when you are working on flat pieces of glass. A reel of masking tape can help to support glass while you are working on it. Use all-purpose strong glue to attach decorations to glass, or to join pieces of acetate.

COTTON BUDS (SWABS) (2)
Use to wipe away painted mistakes, and to remove chinagraph pencil (china marker) marks.

CRAFT KNIFE (3)
Use for cutting templates or stencils from paper, cardboard or sticky-backed plastic.

CUTTING MAT (4)
This will protect your work surface when using a craft knife.

METAL RULER (5)
Use to guide your hand when drawing straight lines, particularly when cutting with a craft knife or when using outliner pens.

NAIL POLISH REMOVER (6)
Before painting, always clean the glass on both sides to remove all traces of grease or fingerprints. Household glass cleaning products can be used but nail polish remover is just as good. Use with paper towels.

PAINTBRUSHES (7)
Always use good-quality artist's paintbrushes in a range of sizes. Clean the brushes as soon as you have finished painting, using water for water-based paints and white spirit (paint thinner) for oil-based paints.

PENCILS AND PENS (8)
Use a pencil or dark-coloured felt-tipped pen when making templates. A chinagraph pencil (china marker) can be used to draw guidelines on the glass and wipes off easily.

SCISSORS (9)
A pair of sharp scissors is useful for cutting sharp curves in a stencil. Use tin snips or heavy scissors to cut the adhesive lead strip.

SPONGE (10)
A natural sponge can be used to give the paint a decorative mottled effect. A synthetic sponge will give a more regular effect. Dampen sponges before use, using water for water-based paints and white spirit (paint thinner) for oil-based paints.

TEASPOON (11)
Use the back of a teaspoon or a boning peg to smooth down the adhesive lead strip to ensure a good contact with the glass.

BASIC TECHNIQUES

If you are new to glass painting, or are trying a technique you have not attempted before, experiment on a spare piece of glass such as a glass jar. If you make a mistake, you can either wipe it away immediately with a cotton bud before the paint begins to dry, or wait until it is completely dry and scrape it off with the blade of a knife.

PREPARING THE GLASS

Clean both sides of the glass to remove any fingermarks or traces of grease before you start to paint, using a special glass cleaner or nail polish remover and a folded paper towel. Do not use white spirit (paint thinner).

TEMPLATES AND STENCILS

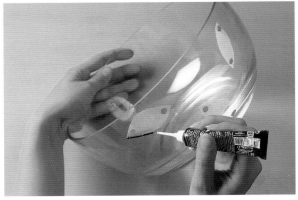

1 If you are working on a flat piece of clear glass, a template can simply be taped to the underside or attached using small pieces of reusable adhesive.

2 When you are decorating a curved surface, such as a bowl, small paper templates can be attached to the inside, following the curve.

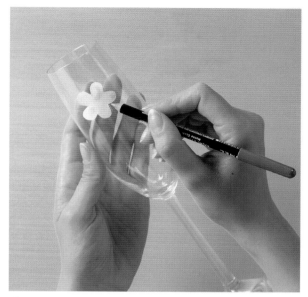

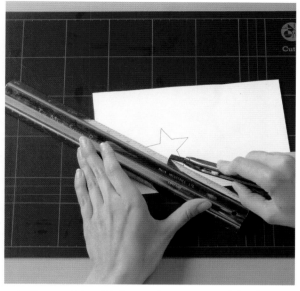

3 When working on a small, curved surface, such as a drinking glass, it may be easier to apply the template to the outside and draw around it using a chinagraph pencil (china marker) to make a guide.

4 Cut straight-sided stencils using a craft knife and a metal ruler and resting on a cutting mat. Always keep your fingers well away from the blade and change the blade frequently to avoid tearing the paper.

5 When you are cutting a stencil which includes tight curves, cut what you can with a craft knife, then use a small pair of sharp-pointed scissors to cut the curves smoothly.

MIXING AND APPLYING PAINT

1 Mix paint colours on a ceramic palette, old plate or tile. To make a light colour, add the colour to white or colourless paint, a tiny amount at a time, until you reach the required shade. Use a separate brush for each colour so that you do not contaminate the paint in the pot.

2 If you want an opaque effect, add a small amount of white glass paint to the transparent coloured paint in the palette.

3 Always use an appropriately-sized paintbrush for the job. A large, flat brush will give a smooth and even coverage over larger areas of glass.

4 Use a very fine brush to paint small details and fine lines. Let one coat of paint dry before painting over it with another colour.

5 To etch a design into the paint, draw into the paint while it is still wet using a toothpick or the other end of the paintbrush. Wipe off the excess paint after each stroke to keep the design clean.

CORRECTING MISTAKES

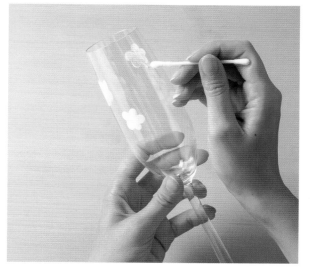

1 Use a cotton bud (swab) to remove a small mistake while the paint is still wet.

2 To remove a larger area of paint, wipe it away immediately using a damp paper towel. If the paint has begun to dry, use nail polish remover.

3 If the paint has hardened completely, small mistakes can be corrected by scraping the paint away using a craft knife

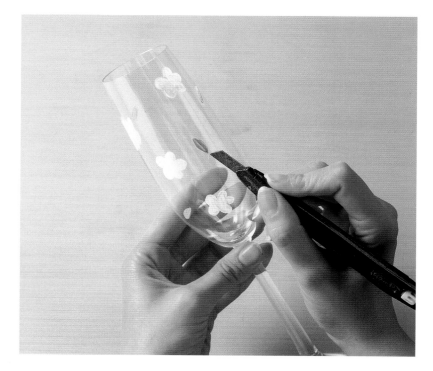

USING RELIEF OUTLINER

1 Practise drawing with outliner on a spare piece of glass. Hold the tube at an angle and drag it smoothly to draw a straight line. If it starts with a blob, this can be removed when dry, using a knife blade.

2 To fill in the outlined shape, wait until the outliner is dry then use a full brush and work around the edge first, then flood the centre.

3 Use outliner to decorate the glass with small dots. Holding the tube at right angles to the glass, touch it gently and lift again, squeezing the tube very lightly.

ADHESIVE LEAD STRIP

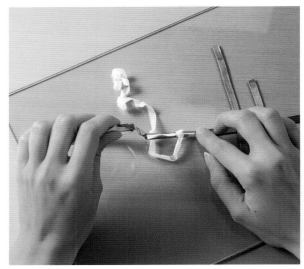

1 Before applying the lead strip, clean the glass thoroughly to remove all traces of grease and fingermarks. Press the strip down gently with your fingers. Always wash your hands after handling lead.

2 It is important that the lead strip is firmly stuck to the glass so that paint will not leak underneath it. After applying the strip, burnish it using a boning peg or the back of an old teaspoon.

APPLYING PAINT WITH A SPONGE

1 Use a dampened natural sponge to achieve a mottled effect. Dip the sponge in the paint then blot it on a sheet of paper to remove the excess paint before applying it to the glass.

2 Use masking tape or reusable adhesive to attach a stencil securely to the glass for sponging.

3 Add texture and interest to sponged decoration by adding a second colour when the first has dried. This is especially effective when both sides of the glass will be visible.

4 Sponge a neat decorative band around a drinking glass by masking off both sides of the band with strips of masking tape.

TEMPLATES

Enlarge the templates on a photocopier. Alternatively, trace the design and draw a grid of evenly spaced squares over your tracing. Draw a larger grid on to another piece of paper and copy the outline square by square. Finally, draw over the lines to make sure they are continuous.

Seashell Lotion Dispenser, pp34–7

Venetiam Perfume Bottle, pp45–7

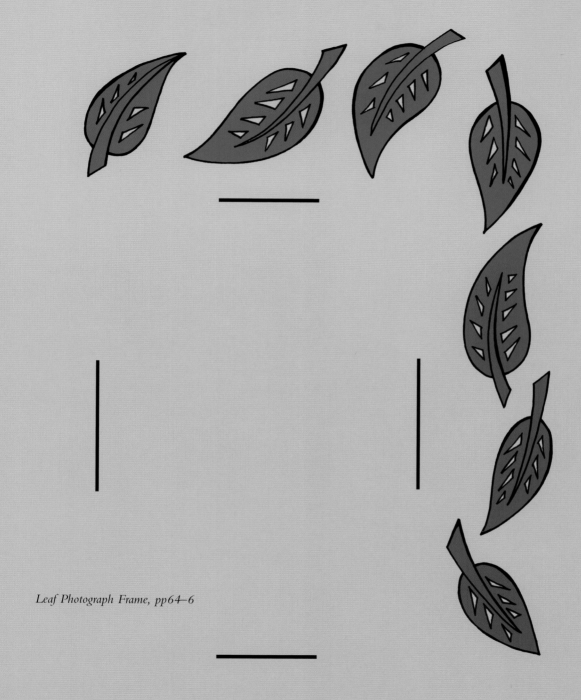

Leaf Photograph Frame, pp64–6

Bohemian Bottle, pp70–2

French-lavender Flower Vase, pp73–5

SUPPLIERS

UNITED KINGDOM
Alec Tiranti Ltd
70 High Street
Theale
Reading
Berkshire RG7 5AR
Tel: (01734) 302 775
*Specialist paints and general
art and craft supplies*

Atlantis Art Materials
146 Brick Lane
London EC1 6RU
Tel: (0171) 377 8855
*Wide selection of art and
craft supplies*

Codu Glassworks
43 Union Street
Maidstone
Kent ME14 1ED
Tel: (01622) 763 615
*Suppliers of glass products
and adhesive lead strip*

Habitat
Tel: (0645) 334 433
*Suppliers of mirrors and
glassware. Call for details
of your nearest branch*

Kernowcraft
Freepost
Bolingey
Perranporth
Cornwall TR6 ODH
Tel: (01872) 573 888
*Suppliers of jeweller's pliers
and fine wire cutters*

Lead and Light
35A Hartland Road
Camden
London NW1 8DB
Tel: (0171) 485 0997
*Suppliers of soldering and
glass-cutting equipment,
etching cream, stained glass,
copper foil and glass paints*

**North Western Lead
  Company Ltd**
Newton Moor Industrial
  Estate
Mill Street
Hyde
Cheshire SK14 4LJ
Tel: (0161) 368 4491
Suppliers of adhesive lead strip

Panduro Hobby
Westward House
Transport Avenue
Brentford
Middlesex TW8 9HF
Tel: (0181) 847 6161

Philip & Tracey Ltd
Tel: (01264) 332 171
*Pébéo Vitrail glass paints are
available from selected art and
craft shops. Call for details of
your nearest stockists*

UNITED STATES
Adventures in Crafts
Yorkville Station
P.O. Box 6058
New York
NY 10128
Tel: (212) 410-0793

Art Supply Warehouse
5325 Departure Drive
North Raleigh
NC 27616
Tel: (919) 878-5077

Craft Catalog
P.O. Box 1069
Reynoldsburg
OH 43068
Tel: (800) 777-1442

Createx Colors
14 Airport Park Road
East Granby
CT 06026
Tel: (860) 653-5505

Creative Craft House
897 San Jose Circle
H.C. 62
P.O. Box 7810
Bullhead City
AZ 864301
Tel: (520) 754-3300

Dick Blick Art Materials
P.O. Box 1267
695 US Highway 150 East
Galesburg
IL 61402
Tel: (309) 343-6181

The Art Store
935 Erie Boulevard E.
Syracuse
NY 13210
Tel: (315) 474-1000

CANADA
Abby Arts & Crafts
4118 Hastings Street
Burnaby
British Columbia
Tel: (604) 299 5201

Lewis Craft
2300 Younge Street
Toronto
Ontario
Tel: (905) 483 2783

Pébéo Canada
1905 Roy Street
Sherbrooke
JIK 2X5
Quebec
Tel: (819) 829 5012

AUSTRALIA
Lincraft
Tel: (03) 9875 7575
Call for details of your nearest store

Pébéo Australia
Tel: (613) 9416 0611
Call for details of your nearest stockist

Spotlight
Tel: freecall 1800 500 021
60 stores throughout Australia

The Stained Glass Centre
221 Hale Street
Peterie Terrace
Queensland 4000
Tel: (02) 8429 1642

The Publishers would like to thank the following artists for the beautiful projects shown in this book: Mary Fellows: Frosted Highball Glasses, Heart Decoration, Celebration Card, Clip Frame, Sugar Shaker, Stained Glass Window, Mosaic Vase; Lucinda Ganderton: Venetian Perfume Bottle, Leaf Photograph Frame, Monogrammed Wine Glass, Bohemian Bottle, French-lavender Flower Vase; Susie Johns: Christmas Baubles, Door Number Plaque, Trinket Box, Mirror; Cheryl Owen: Champagne Flutes, Butterfly Bowl, Seashell Lotion Dispenser, Glass Jar Lantern.

Thanks are also due to Sarah Raine for her help in the studio.

INDEX